Kiwiana
Party Cakes

HarperCollins*Publishers*

First published 2010
HarperCollins*Publishers* (New Zealand) Limited
PO Box 1, Auckland, 1140

Reprinted 2011

HarperCollins*Publishers*
31 View Road, Glenfield, Auckland 0627, New Zealand
25 Ryde Road, Pymble, Sydney, NSW 2073, Australia
A 53, Sector 57, Noida, UP, India
77–85 Fulham Palace Road, London W6 8JB, United Kingdom
2 Bloor Street East, 20th floor, Toronto, Ontario M4W 1A8, Canada
10 East 53rd Street, New York, NY 10022, USA

National Library of New Zealand Cataloguing-in-Publication Data

Burns, Rob, 1963-
Kiwiana party cakes / Rob Burns, Jane Turner and Charlie Smith.
ISBN 978-1-86950-758-9
1. Cake. 2. Cake decorating. I. Turner, Jane, 1940-
II. Smith, Charlie (Charlie Douglas) Ill. Title.
641.8653—dc 22

Design and setting by Carolyn Lewis

Printed by Bookbuilders, China

Kiwiana
Party Cakes

Fun cakes for fun occasions

Rob Burns — *pâtissier*
Photography by Charlie Smith

HarperCollins*Publishers*

Rob Burns

As a 13-year-old schoolboy, Rob worked as a kitchen hand and always knew he wanted to become a chef. He gained his catering qualifications at the Auckland Technology Institute and went to work at Auckland's prestigious Number 5 restaurant. The need to learn more about pastries, desserts and baking took him to England where he gained his City & Guilds Certificate in Pastry and was among the top 10 students in his year. His OE included stints at a Michelin-starred hotel and as head chef at a well-known catering company. Back home in Auckland, Eve's Pantry honed his baking skills, then, as a bakery adviser for NZ Bakels, Rob trained individuals in the industry. Since buying his own patisserie in 2006 in Ponsonby, Rob has developed his love of turning cakes and pastries into nothing less than art forms.

Charlie Smith

After 15 years working as an art director in London ad agencies, Charlie moved to New Zealand and decided to work behind the camera. He now specialises in food photography and was awarded the NZ Best Cookbook Photography in the Gourmand World Cookbook Awards 2009.

Introduction

You can't have a celebration without a cake, and our country is full of iconic images that tug at the heart of every Kiwi. Put the two together and the result is *Kiwiana Party Cakes*. Pastry chef and baker Robert Burns of Rob's Patisserie in Auckland's Ponsonby has created 33 cake designs that look impressive yet are simple to make at home. Using just eight basic cake mixes and with his inventive eye for embellishment, Rob presents home-grown favourites such as a kiwifruit, a sheep, a pair of jandals and a rugby jersey, as well as lolly-lavished numerals for children's birthdays. *Kiwiana Party Cakes*' easy-to-follow instructions and evocative photographs make party cake-making at home — well — a piece of cake!

Acknowledgments

Thanks to Helena Robben, Pip Duncan, Youshka Brandt and the team at Rob's Patisserie.

Suppliers

Decor Cakes, Otahuhu, Auckland, (09) 276 6676
New World supermarkets
Starline Distributors, Wellington, (04) 385 7424
Spotlight

Contents

A Kiwifruit Cake

You will need:

two medium-sized round green cakes
(recipes pages 82–86)

cocoa powder

coconut

chocolate lamington dip
(recipe page 79)

soft icing
(recipe page 78)
coloured yellow and green

chocolate hail

① Bake the cakes in two same-sized, greased, round mixing bowls; cool completely.

② Add the sifted cocoa powder to the coconut and fold together until well mixed.

③ Dunk the rounded sides of each cake into the lamington dip, cover with the cocoa/coconut mixture and leave to set.

④ Place one cake on a board; position the other cake on top with the two non-coated sides together. Cut away half of the top cake.

⑤ Remove both pieces of cut cake. Spread green icing over the top of the bottom cake and replace one half of the cut cake on top.

⑥ Cover the exposed side of the top cake with a liberal amount of green icing.

⑦ Mix a little yellow icing into the green where the two cakes join.

⑧ Before the icing sets, carefully sprinkle chocolate hail to look like kiwifruit seeds.

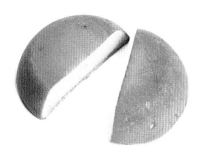

Fit for a Princess

You will need:

one cone-shaped cake
(baked in a special mould —
recipes pages 82–86)

soft white icing
(recipe page 78), some
coloured pink and yellow

ready-to-roll icing coloured
purple

a Barbie doll

two piping bags

two medium-sized star
nozzles

cachous

1. Place the cake on a board and cut a hole in the top big enough to hold the doll.
2. Wrap the bottom half of the doll in plastic wrap and push her into the hole.
3. Cover the entire cake with soft pink icing.
4. With soft white icing, pipe a row of stars around the base of the cake. Change to the second piping bag and pink icing and pipe another row of stars above the first. Continue in alternating white and pink stripes to cover the whole skirt.
5. Finish with a row of pink or silver cachous pushed into the icing around the waist.
6. Dust the bench with icing sugar and cut out little flowers from the purple icing.
7. Push flowers into the soft icing at intervals over the skirt, pipe a small dot of yellow soft icing into the middle of each and finish with a silver cachou.

All Aboard!

You will need:

one medium-sized
square cake
(recipes pages 82–86)

butter cream
(recipe page 78)

ready-to-roll icing coloured
grey, yellow, light blue,
black, white and red

soft white icing
(recipe page 78)

a small piping bag

1. Cut the cake into four strips. Sandwich each strip with butter cream to make four layers. Spread butter cream over the sides and top.
2. Dust the bench with icing sugar and roll out enough grey icing to cover the cake.
3. Roll out enough yellow icing to fit the front end of the cake, brushing with a little water to make it stick.
4. Roll out light blue icing thinly and cut into four strips to make windows. Attach these with a little water.
5. Roll out black icing thickly and cut a rectangle for the front window, three discs for engine fans on the roof and 14 circles for wheels. Roll three oval pieces for the fender. Place these on the cake as shown.
6. For the eyes, roll two balls of white icing, two slightly smaller of light blue and two even smaller of black. Flatten them all a little and press together. Make eyelids from a flattened ball of white icing cut in half. Attach eyes to the front window as shown.
7. Cut red icing into a mouth shape and attach under the front window.
8. Make front lights by rolling two small balls of red icing and two larger balls of white icing into the shapes shown and attach them above the window.
9. Using the soft white icing, pipe a silver fern design on the roof.

Little Brown Kiwi

You will need:

one medium-sized
round cake
(recipes pages 82–86)

one smaller round cake
(recipes pages 82–86)

chocolate butter cream
(recipe page 78)

ready-to-roll icing
coloured yellow, brown,
white and black

chocolate Flake bars

① Make the beak from yellow icing shaped like a long skinny parsnip. Make the feet from two balls of yellow icing flattened slightly into tear drops. Divide the broad ends into three, shaping each toe with your fingers.

② Dust the bench with icing sugar and roll out enough brown icing to cover the top of the smaller cake. At the same time cut three small discs, two for eyes and one to cut in half for eyelids.

③ To assemble the eyes, cut white icing into two larger discs and black icing into two smaller discs. Place a black disc on top of a brown on top of a white and finish with the eyelids, using a little water to hold the pieces in place.

④ Sandwich the smaller cake on top of the larger with butter cream and cover both with more butter cream.

⑤ Cover the top of the smaller cake with the rolled brown icing to make the face.

⑥ Break up the chocolate Flake bars and use them to cover all the butter cream on both cakes.

⑦ Pipe a border of butter cream around the edge of the face.

⑧ Attach the feet to the front of the cake with a little butter cream. Attach the eyes with a little water. Position the beak on top of the cake between the eyes and the feet.

Little Bo Sheep

You will need:

one medium-sized
round cake
(recipes pages 82–86)

one small round cake
(recipes pages 82–86)

pink butter cream
(recipe page 78)

ready-to-roll icing coloured
white, pink, blue, skin-
tone, red and black

pink and white
marshmallows

melted chocolate

① Make the ears and hair bow the previous day. Dust the work surface with icing sugar. For the ears, take two same-sized pieces of white icing and mould each into an oval. Use about half this amount of pink icing to mould smaller ovals; place them on top of the white and secure by brushing with a little water. Gently smooth the tops of the two colours and curl into the desired shape. Place the ears over something round (the bottom of a glass works well) to keep them in shape while they dry.

② For the hair bow, roll out pink icing to 3 mm thickness; trim into a rectangle about 20 cm long and 4 cm wide. Loop both ends to meet in the middle, using the handle of a wooden spoon to support the loops while they dry. Cut a small disc of pink icing and secure this to the join with a little water.

③ To assemble, level the top of the larger cake and place it on a cake board. Spread butter cream over the top and sides. Place the smaller cake on top and towards the front of the larger cake and cover it with more butter cream.

④ To make Little Bo's face, roll out the skin-coloured icing to no more than 3 mm thickness and lay it over the top of the small cake. Trim off any excess, leaving small areas of butter cream exposed at the back; insert the two ears into these.

⑤ Cut one round disc from the skin-coloured icing and cut this in half for eyelids.

⑥ For the eyes, roll out small amounts of white, blue and black icing and cut two discs in gradually decreasing sizes from each colour. Arrange the eyes on the face and secure all layers of colour with a little water. Add the eyelids to the top of the eyes.

⑦ Shape the tongue by hand from a small piece of red icing. Make a small incision in the front of the cake and press the tongue into place.

⑧ Push the back edge of a bread and butter knife into the icing on the face to make an impression for the nose.

⑨ Starting at the bottom edge of the larger cake, push marshmallows into the butter cream in rows until the cake is completely covered.

⑩ To make the feet, cut four marshmallows in half, place the two halves side by side and dip halfway into melted chocolate. When the chocolate has set, arrange the feet in place.

Fly the Flag

You will need:

one medium-sized
oblong cake
(recipes pages 82–86)

butter cream
(recipe page 78)

ready-to-roll icing
coloured royal blue,
white, red and black

white chocolate

four star moulds

① Melt enough white chocolate to fill the star moulds. Allow to set then turn out onto paper. Cut four discs from red icing and attach to the top of the stars. Pipe on smiley faces with melted white chocolate and make eyes from small balls of black icing.

② Spread the cake with butter cream.

③ Roll out enough blue icing to cover the cake. Smooth on carefully as it needs to be really flat.

④ Roll out a thick square of white icing and four strips of red. Form two wide red strips into a cross with two narrow strips in between and place on top of the white icing; cut around the edges. Place on the top left-hand corner of the cake and arrange the stars as shown.

Busy Bees

You will need:

three round cakes in
gradually diminishing sizes
(recipes pages 82–86)

butter cream
(recipe page 78)

ready-to-roll icing
coloured yellow,
dark brown and black

chocolate bees

1. Spread butter cream on top of each cake and stack from largest to smallest.
2. Use a knife to smooth the stack into a beehive shape.
3. Cover the entire cake with butter cream.
4. Dust the bench with icing sugar and roll the yellow icing into ropes long enough to fit around the cake. Wrap three around the first layer of cake, making sure any joins are at the back.
5. Roll the dark brown icing into similar ropes and place one above the third yellow row.
6. Repeat the last two steps for the second and third layers of cake.
7. Top the cake with yellow icing, finishing in a spiral.
8. Make a door shape from black icing and attach to the front of the cake with a little water.
9. Attach chocolate bees with dabs of butter cream.

A Bird in the Hand

You will need:

one cone-shaped cake
(baked in a special mould
— recipes pages 82–86)

butter cream
(recipe page 78)

ready-to-roll icing coloured
blue, red, black and white

a heart-shaped cutter

a sieve

① Make the pukeko's head, beak, eyes and feet the day before. Assemble the cake and leave to dry overnight.

② Use blue icing to make a slight tear-drop shape for the head; the longer end will become the bottom of the beak.

③ Shape the beak around your finger using red icing and attach it to the head with a little water; make two small incisions for the nose holes. Use more red icing to mould and flatten a small piece to attach to the head at the top of the beak.

④ Make the eyes from two balls of blue icing with smaller balls of white and black icing flattened onto them.

⑤ To make the feet, roll six lengths of red icing and squeeze them into claw shapes, using the back of a blunt knife to make skin-like indents. Make two balls of red icing and attach to the feet.

⑥ Place the cake on a board and cover with butter cream.

⑦ Dust the bench with icing sugar and roll out enough blue icing to cover the cake, smoothing and moulding it with your hands. Trim away any excess icing from the base.

⑧ Use a heart-shaped cutter to cut approximately 25 pieces of black icing for wing feathers.

⑨ Starting at the bottom of the pukeko's body, attach the feathers with a little water, leaving a space for tail feathers. Continue until you reach the neck.

⑩ Use a little water to attach the head at the top of the feathers and place the feet facing up.

⑪ To make the tail feathers, push white icing through a large sieve, making the strands as long as possible. Run a blunt knife over the outside of the sieve to lift off the strands and gently place them in the space left at the back of the body.

Play the Game

You will need:

two round cakes
(recipes pages 82–86)

butter cream
(recipe page 78)

ready-to-roll white icing

soft black icing
(recipe page 78)

① Sandwich the two cakes together with butter cream.

② Use a knife to round the top.

③ Cover the entire cake with more butter cream.

④ Dust the bench with icing sugar and roll out enough white icing to cover the cake. Place the icing on top of the butter cream, using your hands to smooth it into place; trim off any excess at the base.

⑤ Use the back of a bread and butter knife to make seam indentations while the icing is still soft.

⑥ Pipe your team's logo or colours into the top panel of the netball.

⑦ Pipe soft black icing into the seam indentations to look like stitching.

It's in the Mail

You will need:

one medium-sized square
or rectangular cake
(recipes pages 82–86)

butter cream
(recipe page 78)

ready-to-roll white icing

a small round cookie-cutter

soft icing
(recipe page 78)
coloured green and red

a piping bag

1. Dust the bench with icing sugar and roll out white icing into a square or rectangle 3 centimetres larger than the cake. Use a small round cookie-cutter to cut away the edges to look like stamp perforations. Cut away the inside to form a border and leave to dry for several hours.
2. Place the cake on a board and cover with butter cream.
3. Roll out enough white icing to cover the cake. Lay the icing over the butter cream and, starting from the top, gently mould it with your hands to fit. Trim off any excess icing from around the base.
4. Pipe an outline of New Zealand on top of the cake with soft green icing and fill in the outline.
5. Pipe the stamp's value and your chosen words with soft red icing.
6. Brush a little water onto the base of the border and attach it to the top of the cake.

On the Slopes

You will need:

two round cakes
(recipes pages 82–86)

butter cream
(recipe page 78)

ready-to-roll icing
coloured white, brown,
yellow and black

soft white icing
(recipe page 78)

1. Make kiwis and skis beforehand and leave the pieces to dry overnight.
2. Roll brown icing into two balls and white icing into two smaller balls. Push one of each colour gently together and roll to join, moulding heads and beaks from the white balls.
3. Cut four skis from yellow icing and curl up one end of each.
4. Make two little caps from black icing.
5. Roll two very small balls of brown icing and two of black and place on top of each other for eyes.
6. When dry, use a little soft white icing to attach the caps to the kiwi heads and add pompoms.
7. Place one cake on a board and cut the second to form the mountain and ski slope. Join the pieces together with butter cream and then cover the entire cake with more butter cream.
8. Dust the bench with icing sugar and roll out enough brown icing to cover the cake. Smooth it on with your hands, trimming away any excess icing from the base.
9. Roll out two strips of white icing and attach these to the skiing slopes, trimming off any excess.
10. Place the kiwis on the slopes.
11. Finish by piping soft white icing to look like snow.

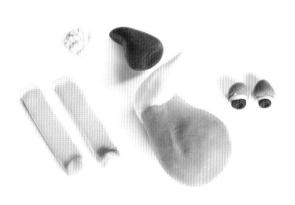

Jaffa Giant

You will need:

two circular cakes
(recipes pages 82–86)

butter cream
(recipe page 78)

ready-to-roll icing coloured
red, white and brown

soft icing coloured red
(recipe page 78)

large and small Jaffas

1. To make a circular cake, bake the cake mixture in two same-sized mixing bowls.
2. Sandwich the two half-rounds together with butter cream, then place on a cake board and cover with more butter cream.
3. Dust the bench with icing sugar and roll out the red icing. Place over the entire cake and mould into shape with your hands.
4. For the eyes, cut two large circles from white icing and two smaller circles from brown. Attach the brown on top of the white with a little water and place on the front of the cake.
5. Cut one circle the same size as the eye whites from red icing and cut in half to make eyelids. Attach these at the top of the eyes with a little water.
6. Roll two pieces of brown icing with your hands to make eyebrows and attach these directly above the eyes with a little water.
7. Roll out a thin rope of brown icing, long enough to make a smile from eye to eye, and place on the cake.
8. Attach one large Jaffa for a nose.
9. Pipe a little soft red icing around the base of the cake and push in Jaffas to make a border.

Make a Splash

You will need:

two round cakes
(recipes pages 82–86)

blue butter cream
(recipe page 78)

ready-to-roll icing coloured
blue, black, brown, pink,
skin-tone and yellow

finger wafers

1. Prepare the figurines the day before. Assemble the cake and leave to dry overnight.
2. Using blue icing, shape the girl's torso. Use skin-toned icing to make a ball for the girl's head, and to shape her arms and legs and the boy's legs.
3. Dust the bench with icing sugar and cut the lilo from pink icing, using the back of a blunt knife to make its indents.
4. Make the boy's shorts by shaping black icing into a rectangle; push in the legs.
5. Make the girl's hat and place it flat over her head.
6. Arrange the girl on the lilo.
7. Assemble the swimming pool by sandwiching the two cakes with a layer of butter cream.
8. Place the cake on a board and cover entirely with blue butter cream, leaving the top a little textured to look like water.
9. Circle the cake with the wafers.
10. Roll a thick rope of blue icing for the rim and base of the pool.
11. Arrange the figurines on the water.

Note: Blue jelly on top of the cake would also look really cool.

Not-so-scary Weta

You will need:

medium-sized oblong cake
(recipes pages 82–86)

butter cream
(recipe page 78)

ready-to-roll icing
coloured light brown,
black, blue, white and red

liquorice tubes

1. Place the cake on a board and cover with butter cream.
2. Dust the bench with icing sugar and roll out enough light brown icing to cover the cake. Mould and smooth the icing over the butter cream, trimming off any excess around the base.
3. Cut four large discs of brown icing for body armour, one smaller disc for the face and an even smaller one cut in half for eyelids.
4. Attach the largest discs along the top of the body, overlapping each slightly. Place the face disc at the front.
5. Roll 12 small balls of brown icing, stack in pairs and press in three groups along each side of the body.
6. Make the weta's feet from six ovals of white icing. Roll a long, thin strip from blue icing and place three pieces over each foot to look like sports shoes.
7. Attach one end of a liquorice tube into each sports shoe, bend each tube and push the other end into the balls stacked at the sides of the body.
8. Slightly flatten two balls of white icing for eyes. Attach two small black balls to the whites and arrange on the face, using a little water to secure the eyelids over the tops of the eyes.
9. Make a small ball of red icing for the nose and flatten onto the face.
10. Use strips of liquorice to make antenna and a little French moustache.

Carrot Feast

You will need:

one medium-sized
rectangular cake
(recipes pages 82–86)

butter cream
(recipe page 78)

soft icing
(recipe page 78)

ready-to-roll icing coloured
grey, white, pink, brown,
orange, dark green, light
green, yellow, red and black

leaf and flower moulds

toothpicks

a sieve

① Make the rabbit body parts, leaves, flowers and tiny carrots the day before. Assemble the cake and leave to dry overnight.

② For each rabbit's body, take a ball of grey icing and another of white about a quarter of the size and flatten both slightly. Put the white on top of the grey and flatten together but keep the body shape rounded.

③ Use the same amount of grey icing for the head, shaping it into a long tear drop and pinching it in the middle to define the ears. Use a blunt knife to make a split from the top of the head to the end of the ears; separate and twist each ear slightly for a natural look. Take two very small balls of pink icing, shape into tear drops, place inside the ears and flatten together.

④ For the whiskers, roll white icing into a small block and use your index finger to gently flatten the middle so it becomes bone-shaped. Press this on to the bottom of the head, pinching the pieces together, and use the back of a blunt knife to score the white piece to look like whiskers.

⑤ Make the arms from rolls of grey icing, flattening and scoring the ends to look like fingers. Pinch into shape more rolls of grey icing for feet, finishing the soles with little dots of white icing as shown.

⑥ For eyes, flatten small balls of black icing over slightly larger balls of white. Flatten a ball of grey icing, cut it in half and attach over the tops of the eyes for eyelids.

⑦ Flatten a small ball of white icing and score it to look like two teeth. Flatten a ball of red icing and attach it above the teeth for a nose.

⑧ Using a mould, make 16 leaves in dark green and 16 in light green icing. Curl each leaf over an index finger for a natural look and leave on a board to dry. Use a mould to make 12 differently coloured little flowers. Make tiny carrots from rolls of orange icing, indenting the tops to take a leaf and scoring the sides with the back of a knife.

9   To assemble the cake, dust a work surface with icing sugar. Roll out brown icing to fit a cake board spread with a little butter cream and trim around the edges of the icing to look like a patch of earth.

10 Cut two same-sized ovals from the cake and sandwich together with a thin layer of butter cream. Use a knife to round off one end and make a slight point at the other to form a carrot shape. Lightly cover the whole cake with butter cream and place it on the earth patch.

11 Roll out enough orange icing to cover the cake, smooth it over with the palm of your hand and trim any excess from the bottom edge. Use the back of a blunt knife to mark the icing into ridges.

12 Cut black icing into a small disc. Place this on the carrot where shown, using a little water to hold it in place.

13 Assemble the rabbits. Use a toothpick to attach a head to each body and attach arms, feet and little carrots with dabs of soft icing. Use more soft icing to hold the rabbits in place around the cake.

14 Arrange the leaves around the base of the cake, securing them in place with soft icing, and add the flowers last.

15 Make the carrot top by pushing a piece of green icing through a large sieve to make the fronds as long as possible. Gently prise them from the back of the sieve with a blunt knife and attach to the top end of the carrot with some soft icing.

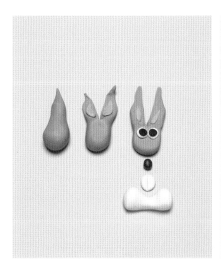

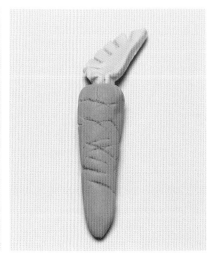

Can't Be Licked

You will need:

two small round cakes
(recipes pages 82–86)

butter cream
(recipe page 78)

pink wafer biscuits

a hokey pokey Crunchie bar

① Sandwich the two cakes with butter cream.

② Place the cake on a board and spread with butter cream, leaving the top half textured to look like ice cream.

③ Cut the wafer biscuits in half, arrange around the base of the cake and press lightly into the butter cream; the last two wafers may need to be trimmed to fit.

④ Break up a Crunchie bar and poke the pieces into the butter cream on top of the cake.

Cop This

You will need:

a large square cake
(recipes pages 82–86)

butter cream
(recipe page 78)

ready-to-roll icing coloured
white, light blue, black,
red, orange and grey

soft icing
(recipe page 78)
coloured light blue,
yellow and white

① Cut the cake into one large rectangle and one smaller piece to sit on top for the cab.

② Place on a board and sandwich the two pieces together with butter cream then cover the entire cake with more butter cream.

③ Dust the bench with icing sugar and roll out enough white icing to cover the cake, smoothing it on with your hands; trim away any excess icing from the base.

④ Cut out windows from black icing: two large rectangles for the front and rear, and two smaller rectangles for each side. Attach with a little water.

⑤ Flatten four small balls of black icing to form tyres. From smaller discs of grey icing, cut out wedges to make spokes and attach these with a little water to the centre of the tyres. Attach to the car.

⑥ To make lights, flatten four small balls of black icing for bases, shape two white balls for headlights and two smaller orange balls for indicators. Use a little water to attach these to the black bases and to the car.

⑦ For the patrol light, make one rectangle of white icing, two balls of red icing and two of light blue and attach all these with water to the roof.

⑧ Add eyes for fun. Cut three large discs from white icing; cut one in half to make eyelids. Cut two smaller discs from light blue icing. Roll two small balls of black icing. Place the blue discs on top of the white, flatten the black balls and press them into the blue and place the lids across the top of the eyes. Use a little water to make all the pieces stick together.

⑨ Make two rolls of grey icing for front and back bumpers and attach to the car with a little water.

⑩ Cut two small rectangles of blue icing and two thin strips of red and attach to each door for police signs.

⑪ Use soft icing to pipe on police signs.

Happy Feet

You will need:

one medium-sized
oblong cake
(recipes pages 82–86)

butter cream
(recipe page 78)

ready-to-roll icing
coloured marbled green,
yellow and pink

a liquorice strap

1. Cut two large flowers from the yellow icing and two smaller flowers from the pink.
2. Cut the cake in half lengthways and shape two identical ovals for the soles of the jandals.
3. Spread each cake with butter cream.
4. Dust the bench with icing sugar, take two same-sized balls of marbled green icing and roll out to cover each cake.
5. Lay the icing over each cake and mould it gently with your hands to fit; trim the excess from the bottom edges.
6. Make three cuts in each jandal to hold the liquorice straps; allow extra length for pushing each strap firmly into the cake.
7. Attach the flowers with a dab of butter cream.

On the Ball

You will need:

two medium-sized square cakes
(recipes pages 82–86)

butter cream
(recipe page 78)

ready-to-roll icing coloured light brown and dark brown

① Sandwich the two cakes with butter cream and cut into a rugby ball shape. Cover with more butter cream.

② Dust the bench with icing sugar and roll out enough light brown icing to cover the cake completely.

③ Roll out an oval of dark brown icing and cut in half. Place one half on each end of the ball (use a little water to make them stick).

④ Press lines with the back of a knife into the sides and top of the cake to represent stitching.

⑤ Make the laces from light brown icing cut into strips. Make five small round holes on either side of the middle seam and attach the laces to these.

One for the Birds

You will need:

one round cake
(recipes pages 82–86)

soft chocolate icing
(recipe page 78)

ready-to-roll icing
coloured blue, light
green and dark green

chocolate finger biscuits

a leaf mould

① Make the fantail's body, wings and tail and the leaves the day before assembling the cake.

② Shape the head and body from one piece of blue icing. Make a slit on either side of the body to hold the wings when they have dried. Flatten two balls of blue icing into ovals for wings and use a blunt knife to score a feather design. Cut separate tail feathers from blue icing and gently squeeze together into a fan shape.

③ Use a mould to make 16 leaves in dark green and 16 in light green icing. Curl each one over an index finger for a natural look and place on a board to dry overnight.

④ To assemble, spread the cake with soft chocolate icing and texture it a little to look like tree bark.

⑤ Arrange the chocolate fingers into a nest in the wet icing, leaving a small space in the middle for the fantail to sit.

⑥ Place the leaves in bunches under and around the chocolate fingers.

⑦ Attach the bird's tail with a little soft icing, gently push the wings into the slits in its body and use tiny dots of icing for eyes. Place the finished fantail in the nest.

Practice Makes Perfect

You will need:

large square cake
(recipes pages 82–86)

butter cream
(recipe page 78)

ready-to-roll icing coloured
yellow, red, green, orange,
blue, black and white

① Place the cake on a board and trim to make a jersey shape
   with sleeves.
② Cover with butter cream.
③ Dust the bench with icing sugar and, starting with one sleeve,
   cut the coloured icings into shapes and lay them over the
   butter cream, working your way across and down the jersey.
   Take care to match joins neatly.
④ Use black icing to make the V-neck.
⑤ Roll and fold white icing to make the collar and attach with a
   little water to the black V already placed on the cake.

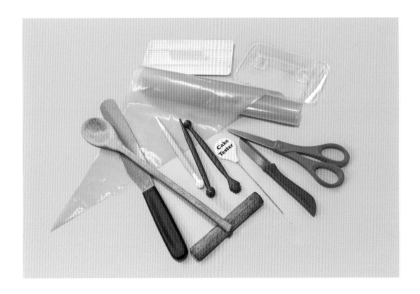

Fish Fatale

You will need:

one medium-sized
square cake
(recipes pages 82–86)

butter cream
(recipe page 78)

ready-to-roll icing
coloured white, orange,
blue, red and black

edible gold powder
(available from a cake-
decorating speciality shop)

a little vodka or gin

a small paintbrush

① Cut the cake into a fish shape, using leftover pieces to make the upper and lower fins. Coat with butter cream.

② Roll out enough white icing to cover the whole cake.

③ Cut orange icing into shapes for the tail and fins and score it as shown. Secure to the white icing with a little water.

④ Thickly roll more white icing and cut out about 20 small circles; cut each in half. Starting at the tail end, place them in overlapping rows to form scales. Leave space for the face.

⑤ Mix the gold powder with a little vodka or gin to make a liquid and paint a thin line along the edge of each scale.

⑥ To make the eye, cut circles of white, blue and black icing, each smaller than the last, and one very small white circle with a V cut out as shown. Make the eyelid from a white circle the same size as that for the eye; cut it in half and place over top of the eye. Press all the circles together to keep them in place. Roll a little strip of black icing to make the eyebrow.

⑦ Make the lips by rolling red icing into two tear-drop shapes and place them on the cake below the eye.

Get Moving

You will need:

two medium-sized
oblong cakes
(recipes pages 82–86)

butter cream
(recipe page 78)

ready-to-roll icing
coloured light blue, yellow,
black, white and grey

sugar flowers for
decorating (optional)

1. Sandwich the two cakes together with a little butter cream, and then coat both cakes with more butter cream.
2. Roll out light blue icing in a wide strip to fit around the bottom cake.
3. Roll out yellow icing to fit the sides and roof of the top cake.
4. Roll a long, thin strip of yellow icing to cover the join between the two colours and another to mark the edge of the roof.
5. Cut black icing into squares for windows.
6. Mould five balls of black icing into tyres. Press grey icing into small spoke shapes and push five into the centre of each tyre.
7. Use light blue icing to shape four mudguards and attach above the tyres as shown.
8. Make headlights from two balls of grey icing and two smaller balls of white. Press them together and attach to the van on either side of the front tyre. Make two small side lights in the same way.
9. Roll out two strips of grey icing to make front and rear bumpers and secure in place with a little water.
10. You may like to give your Kombi some flower power by decorating it all over with colourful little flowers.

Teddies' Cubby House

You will need:

gingerbread dough
(recipe page 84)

soft icing
(recipe page 78)

assorted lollies

Tiny Teddy biscuits

hundreds and thousands

a piping bag

① Dust the bench with flour and roll out gingerbread dough to a thickness of 5 mm. Make four same-sized panels for a square house or two short panels and two longer ones for a rectangular house.

② With the back of a blunt knife, score deep grooves in the dough to look like planks with smaller, shallower grooves to add wood-grain detail.

③ Cut out space for a door from the front panel and use some of the trimmings to make a door frame; attach this around the opening.

④ To make the roof, roll out dough to twice the length of the front panel and trim the edges. Pull and fold the dough to make it look corrugated.

⑤ Roll out dough for the floor and score this to look like wood.

⑥ Bake all the panels at 180°C for 25–35 minutes, until firm to the touch. They can be made several days in advance and left to dry out.

⑦ Before assembling, fill the grooves between wooden planks with brightly coloured soft icing to look like grouting on a log house; leave to dry. Spread a little soft icing between the roof corrugations and sprinkle with hundreds and thousands.

⑧ Use soft icing to stick all the pieces together. Start by piping icing on to the base of the wall panels and set these in place on the floor. Pipe more icing behind each panel where it joins the floor and down all of the adjoining wall edges.

⑨ Use heavy objects (such as boxes or cans) to prop up the walls while the icing sets; this can take several hours.

⑩ Attach the roof with more icing piped along the top edge of each wall.

⑪ Decorating the house is the fun part so involve the children; use soft icing to attach all the lollies and Tiny Teddies.

Feel the Buzz

You will need:

two small round cakes
(recipes pages 82–86)

butter cream
(recipe page 78)

ready-to-roll icing
coloured yellow, black,
blue, white and red

liquorice

① Make the paddles, wheels and antenna the day before. Assemble the cake and leave to dry.

② Use yellow icing to make two round shapes for paddles plus a length of thick rope. While the icing is still soft, cut the rope into two equal lengths and make a horizontal slit at one end of both pieces. Gently push a paddle through each slit and press it into place. (This part is easier to handle in two pieces.)

③ Use blue icing to make two wheels the same size and shape as the paddles. Roll two small balls of red icing with your hands and push one into the middle of each wheel.

④ For the antenna, cut two small lengths of liquorice and push a small ball of red icing on to one end of each.

⑤ To assemble, trim each cake into shape for the body and head, and sandwich together with a little butter cream; spread more butter cream over the entire surface.

⑥ Dust the bench with icing sugar and roll out enough red icing to cover the body half of the cake.

⑦ Roll out the yellow icing to cover the other half for the face.

⑧ From the black icing, cut a triangular piece to fit on top of the head; attach with a little water.

⑨ Roll two balls of red icing in your hands for spacers between the wheels and the body. Place on either side where the body and head join and squeeze into place. Attach each wheel to a red ball with a little water.

⑩ Place both paddles on the join where the red and yellow body parts meet, resting on the wheels, and push the two separate pieces together in the middle. Use a little water to hold them in place.

⑪ Make stripes for the top of the body by rolling two small yellow and black icing ropes between your palms and flattening them together. Attach with a little water.

⑫ To make the eyes, take two balls of white icing and two smaller balls of black. Place a black ball on top of a white, flatten together and place on the face with a little water.

⑬ Make two very small black ropes for eyebrows and attach above the eyes.

⑭ Make the mouth from a small flat piece of black icing shaped into a smile with a tiny dot of red icing for a tongue.

⑮ Push the antenna into the black icing on the head.

Faithful Friend

You will need:

one medium-sized
round cake
(recipes pages 82–86)

one small round cake
(recipes pages 82–86)

butter cream
(recipe page 78)

ready-to-roll icing
coloured brown, white,
blue, red and black

1. Cut a circle out of the smaller cake to form the dog's nose and trim the remaining pieces for raised eyebrows.
2. Attach these to the larger cake with butter cream then spread the entire cake with more butter cream.
3. Dust the bench with icing sugar and roll out enough brown icing to cover the sides and part of the top of the cake, leaving the nose and eyebrows exposed. Smooth the icing with your hands, trimming away any excess from the base.
4. Roll out a circle of white icing and mould this over the nose and eyebrows, extending it to meet the brown icing at the edges of the face.
5. Cut three large discs from white icing, two for the eyes and one cut in half for eyelids. Cut two smaller discs from blue icing and place these on top of the white. Finish with two small black icing discs and press them all together. Attach to the face with the eyelids, using a little water to make them stick.
6. Shape the mouth and eyebrows from a thin roll of brown icing.
7. Cut out two long ovals from brown icing to make ears and mould them on to the back of the raised eyebrows, bending them a little to give the dog character.
8. Cut dots of brown icing for nose whiskers and a larger disc of brown for the tip of the nose; attach these pieces with a little water.
9. Shape red icing into a tongue, mark a groove down the middle and let it drape a little.

A Prickly Customer

You will need:

one chocolate sponge roll
(recipe page 86)

soft chocolate icing
(recipe page 78)

ready-to-roll white icing

two giant wine gums

two soft sugar jubes

a piping bag and a
star nozzle

① Place the sponge roll on a board.

② Half-fill the piping bag with soft chocolate icing and, starting from the middle of the top, pipe a row of stars along the length of the roll. Continue piping one row on each side until the log is completely covered.

③ Pipe a swirl of soft chocolate icing around each end of the roll.

④ To make the eyes, cut two large discs of white icing and place them on one end of the roll. Attach a wine gum to the middle of each with a dab of chocolate icing and centre those with a dot of icing for pupils.

⑤ Attach one jube for a nose and another for a mouth.

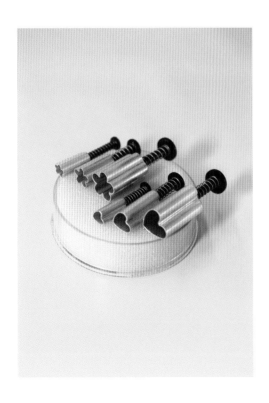

Happy Birthday

You will need:

one round cake
(recipes pages 82–86)

soft chocolate icing
(recipe page 78)

a palette knife

a piping bag and
a star nozzle

soft white icing
(recipe page 78)

a small paper piping bag

① When preparing the chocolate icing, add a few extra drops of water to make it softer to help spread the icing over the cake.

② Using a palette knife, spread the soft icing roughly over the top and the side of the cake.

③ Smooth the top of the cake by using the flat edge of the palette knife, bringing it backwards and forwards over the cake until a smooth surface is achieved. The smoothing of the icing is made much easier if the palette knife is wiped clean after each swipe.

④ Ensure the palette knife is clean and use it to swipe the side of the cake to make it smooth. As before, clean the palette knife after each smoothing stroke.

⑤ Decoration around the side of the cake can be applied next, by taking handfuls of your chosen decoration and pressing it to the icing on the side of the cake.

⑥ Place the star nozzle in the piping bag and half fill the piping bag with chocolate icing. Pipe a decorative border around the crown of the cake.

⑦ Use 1 tablespoon of soft white icing and add a couple of drops of water to make it softer for piping. Using a small paper piping bag (see below), write a 'Happy Birthday' message.

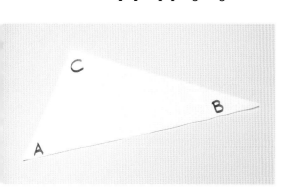

How to make a small paper piping bag

① Take a small triangle of greaseproof paper and label each corner of the triangle: the top of the triangle will be labelled C and the other two corners will be labelled A and B, with AB the longest side.

② Holding corner C in your fingertips, grab corner A and bring it up and turn under to corner C, making a half cone.

③ Still holding C and A together, turn the half cone over and with your other hand, take corner B and bring it up and turn under to join C and A.

④ All three corners should meet to form a perfect cone and the hole at the cone point will be small.

⑤ Fold over all three corners C, A and B and press to hold the cone together, or use a piece of sticky tape.

⑥ Half fill the cone with softened icing; fold the top edge over two or three times to secure the icing in the cone.

⑦ Snip off the tip and gently squeeze to check the flow and thickness for the writing.

You're Number One

You will need:

square cake
(recipes pages 82–86)

ready-to-roll icing
coloured orange

orange butter cream
(recipe page 78)

lots of Pebbles

a piping bag

① Start by covering a cake board. Dust the bench with icing sugar and roll out orange icing to fit the board, trimming any excess from around the edges.

② Cut the cake in half and sandwich the two halves with butter cream; place on top of the iced cake board.

③ Spread the cake all over with more butter cream and pipe a border around the bottom.

④ Press rows of Pebbles into each side of the cake and as a border around the top.

Fab Four

You will need:

one square cake
(recipes pages 82–86)

yellow butter cream
(recipe page 78)

a packet of Pineapple Lumps

① Cut the cake into strips of the same width and assemble as shown into a number four.

② Join the pieces together with butter cream and then cover the whole cake with more butter cream.

③ Press a border of Pineapple Lumps into the butter cream around the edge.

④ Completely cover the top of the cake with Pineapple Lumps, cutting them to fit where necessary.

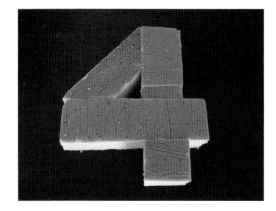

Catch of the Day

You will need:

one small square cake
(recipes pages 82–86)

one small round cake
(recipes pages 82–86)

pink butter cream
(recipe page 78)

two packets mini
chocolate fish

①   Cut the cakes and assemble as shown into a number five.

②   Join the pieces together with butter cream and cover the whole cake with more butter cream.

③   Arrange a border of chocolate fish around the edges.

Ready for Take-off

You will need:

one square cake
(recipes pages 82–86)

green butter cream
(recipe page 78)

a little ready-to-
roll white icing

one packet jet planes

① Cut the cake into strips and assemble as shown into a
number seven.
② Join the pieces together with butter cream and cover the
whole cake with more butter cream.
③ Cut the white icing into small rectangles and thin strips
for runway markings as shown.
④ Place a border of jet planes around the edge of the cake
and arrange more on top.

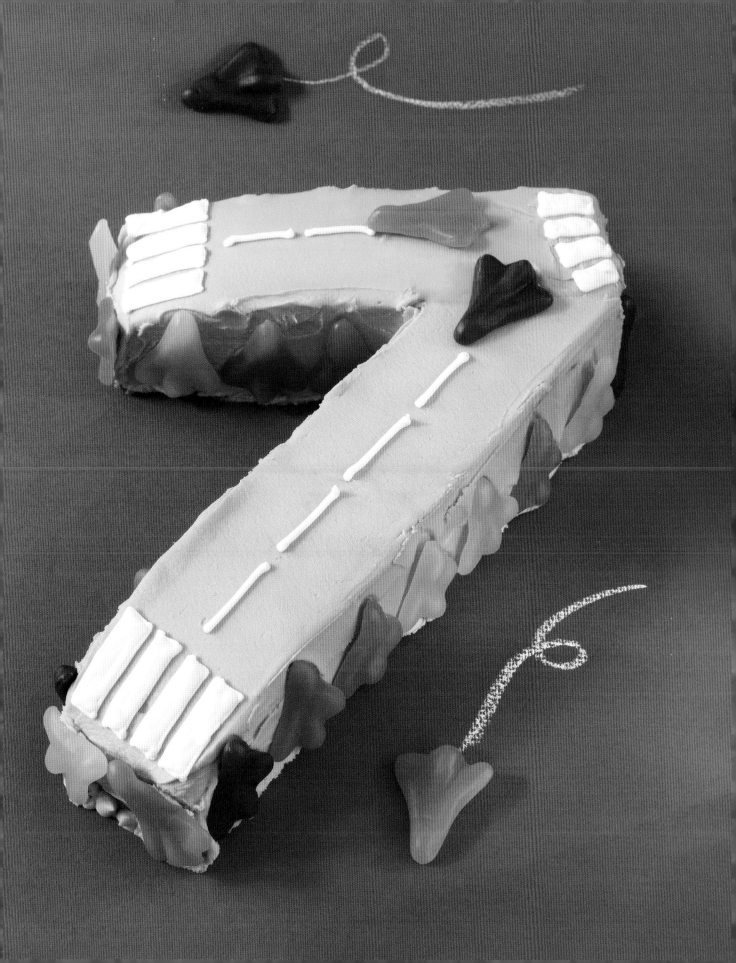

Good Enough to Bottle

You will need:

two same-sized round cakes
(recipes pages 82–86)

blue butter cream
(recipe page 78)

one packet milk bottle lollies

① Cut the cakes as shown to make a number eight.

② Join the two pieces together with butter cream and then cover the whole cake with more butter cream.

③ Place a border of milk bottles around the edges.

④ Starting at a join, arrange milk bottles evenly in a single row around the top of the cake.

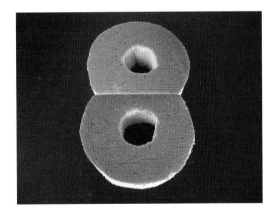

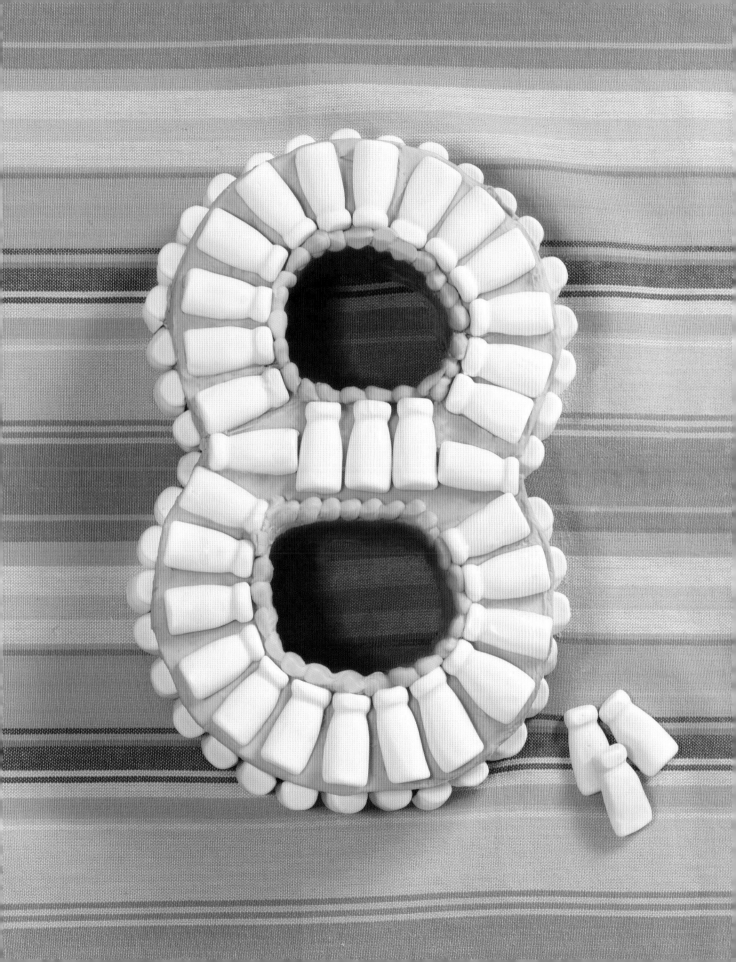

Icings/Colour Mix

ICINGS

Butter Cream
This soft, creamy mixture can be used as a filling between layers of any cake and to join pieces of cake together. Spread thinly all over a cake, it will help to fill any holes or gaps and make a smooth surface for ready-to-roll icing.

125g softened butter
1 tablespoon warm milk
flavouring of your choice
375g icing sugar

Put the butter, milk and any flavouring in a mixing bowl. Sift in the icing sugar a little at a time and beat well between each addition until it has all been incorporated and the mixture is light and creamy.

Makes 500g — enough to cover one cake.

Soft Icing
Use this to spread over a cake or put in a piping bag for decorating.

100g softened butter
2 tablespoons warm water
380g (2½ cups) icing sugar

Beat the butter and water until creamy; slowly add the icing sugar until well combined. If the mixture is a little stiff, add a few more drops of water.

Makes 500g — enough to cover one cake.

Variations

Chocolate:	add 1 tablespoon cocoa
Coffee :	dissolve 1 teaspoon instant coffee in the water
Lemon:	use juice instead of water
Orange:	use juice instead of water

Chocolate Lamington Dip

450g (4 cups) icing sugar
30g (⅓ cup) cocoa
3 tablespoons butter
120ml (½ cup) boiling water

Put all the ingredients in a bowl large enough to hold a cake for dipping. Mix thoroughly until there are absolutely no lumps. Use the mixture while it is still warm.

Colouring Icing

Experimenting with food colouring is fun. One drop is enough for basic colours but here are a few combinations to increase the range.

Deep yellow: 2 drops yellow, 1 drop red
Lime green: 3 drops yellow, 1 drop green
Forest green: 4 drops blue, 1 drop red, 1 drop yellow
Purple: 1 drop blue, 2 drops red
Orange: 1 drop red, 3 drops yellow
Skin-tone: using prepared icing, mould together 100g white icing, 100g orange icing and 5g red icing as shown below
Marbled green: using prepared icing, mould together 100g white icing and 100g green icing as shown below

Icing Made for Rolling

Ready-to-roll icing can be found in the baking aisles of some supermarkets. It costs more than icing sugar but is foolproof because all you have to do is add colour and roll it out — it's like playing with play dough. Be sure, however, to keep each colour wrapped tightly in plastic film to stop it from drying out.

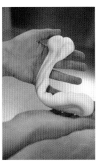

Decorations

Basic Cake Recipes

Butter (Madeira) Cake

250g butter
250g sugar
4 large eggs
250g self-raising flour
125g plain flour
4 teaspoons lemon juice

Preheat the oven to 180°C. Grease and line a 23-cm cake tin with baking paper.
Cream the butter and sugar together until light and fluffy.
Add the eggs one at a time and beat well after each addition.
Sift the flours together and fold into the creamed mixture.
Fold in the lemon juice.
Pour the mixture into the prepared tin and bake for 40 minutes or until a skewer inserted in the middle comes out clean.

Carrot Cake

250g flour
2 teaspoons baking powder
1 teaspoon baking soda
2 teaspoons cinnamon
1 teaspoon allspice
1 teaspoon nutmeg
275g grated carrot
350g sugar
150ml sunflower oil
4 large eggs
75g raisins
75g walnuts
75g chopped pineapple

Preheat the oven to 180°C. Grease and line a 23-cm cake tin with baking paper.
Sift the flour, baking powder, baking soda and spices into a large mixing bowl. Add all the other ingredients and mix until well combined.
Pour the mixture into the prepared tin and bake for 45 minutes or until a skewer inserted in the middle comes out clean.

Chocolate Cake

300g softened butter
250g sugar
4 large eggs
1 teaspoon vanilla essence
500g self-raising flour
3 tablespoons cocoa powder
150ml milk

Preheat the oven to 170°C. Grease and line a 20-cm cake tin with baking paper.
Cream the butter and sugar until light and fluffy.
Add the eggs one at a time, beating well after each addition, then add the vanilla.
Sift the flour and cocoa together and fold alternately with the milk into the creamed mixture.
Pour the mixture into the prepared tin and bake for 40 minutes or until a skewer inserted in the middle comes out clean.

Fruit Cake

700g mixed fruit (raisins, sultanas, currants)
125g mixed peel
125g glacé cherries
3 tablespoons flour
250g softened butter
250g sugar
5 large eggs
250g sifted flour
2 teaspoons baking powder
2 teaspoons mixed spice
2 teaspoons nutmeg
pinch of salt

Preheat oven to 150°C. Grease and line a 20-cm cake tin with baking paper.
Place the mixed fruit, peel and cherries in a bowl and fold through the 3 tablespoons of flour. (This will ensure the fruit is evenly dispersed when the cake is baked.)
Cream the butter and sugar until light and fluffy. Add the eggs one at a time, beating well after each addition.
Sift the dry ingredients together and add to the mixture; stir thoroughly.
Gently fold in the floured fruit.
Pour the mixture into the prepared tin and smooth the top. Bake for 2–2½ hours or until a skewer inserted in the middle comes out clean.
Take the cake out of the oven and leave it to cool in the tin, covered with a towel to keep it moist.

Gingerbread

80g butter
120g golden syrup
160g brown sugar
2 large eggs
450g flour
1 tablespoon ground ginger
¼ teaspoon baking soda

Melt the butter and golden syrup in a large saucepan.
Add the remaining ingredients and mix until it forms a ball of dough. Wrap the ball in plastic wrap and chill in the fridge for 1 hour.
Heat the oven to 180°C. Line a baking tray with baking paper.
On a floured bench roll out the dough to a thickness of 4mm and cut shapes as desired.
Bake for 25–35 minutes or until evenly browned.

Gluten-free Chocolate Cake

160g Healtheries Simple Wheat & Gluten-Free Baking Mix
50g cocoa powder
1 teaspoon gluten-free baking powder
120g ground almonds
150g sugar
3 large eggs
150ml water
150ml sunflower oil
120g sour cream
100g chocolate chips (optional)

Preheat the oven to 160°C. Grease and line a 21-cm cake tin with baking paper.
Sift together the Healtheries Baking Mix, cocoa powder and baking powder. Add the ground almonds and stir until well combined.
Whisk together the remaining ingredients for 1 minute.
Fold in the dry ingredients and blend for a further 4 minutes.
Pour the mixture into the prepared tin and bake for 40 minutes.

Mud Cake

250ml milk
250g softened butter
100ml canola or sunflower oil
4 large eggs
125ml (1 teacup) strong cold coffee
2 dessertspoons golden syrup
350g caster sugar
500g self-raising flour
1 teaspoon baking soda
125g cocoa powder

Preheat the oven to 160°C. Grease and line a 21-cm cake tin with baking paper.
Put the milk, butter, oil, eggs, coffee, golden syrup and sugar in a mixing bowl and whisk until combined.
Sift the flour, baking soda and cocoa and add to the liquid mixture.
Mix to a smooth batter.
Pour the mixture into the prepared tin and bake for 1 hour or until a skewer inserted in the middle comes out clean.

Sponge Cake

3 large eggs
175g sugar
pinch of salt
65g flour
65g cornflour
1 teaspoon baking powder
50g butter
2 tablespoons boiling water

Preheat the oven to 190°C. Grease a deep 20-cm cake tin.
Beat the eggs until foamy.
Add the sugar and salt and beat until thick and creamy — this will take up to 10 minutes.
Fold in the sifted flour, cornflour and baking powder.
Melt the butter in the hot water and fold into the mixture.
Pour the mixture into the prepared tin and bake for 30 minutes.

NOTE: The lengthy beating of the eggs is really important. Do not be tempted to beat for less than 10 minutes or the resulting sponge will not be miraculously light and fluffy.

Sponge Roll

Use the same ingredients as for the sponge cake.

Preheat the oven to 190°C. Grease and lightly flour a swiss roll tin.
Spread the batter evenly in the prepared tin and bake for 10 minutes or until slightly golden.
While still warm, turn the sponge out of the tin onto greaseproof paper that has been sprinkled with caster sugar.
Roll up the sponge and the paper together into a log; leave to cool.
When cold, unroll the log and remove the paper. Spread the sponge with jam and roll up again, making sure the end is underneath to keep the log from unrolling.